Islands

Of

Disbelief

Judith Steele

Reprobate / GobQ Books, Portland, Oregon
2022

My grandfather climbed a
giant's tower at Osborne.
My grandfather made the
sun.

praise for **JUDITH STEELE**'s **iSLANDS**

> Some of these poems cut like a knife into the undulating center of a waterbed. Others make myths of the mundane—first days of school, washing dirty nappies, growing old. Steele's work is humming and alive. Like the konjaks of Kupang, she says, "Let's go."
>
> – Brenda Taulbee, author,
> *The Art of Waking Up*

F DiSBELiEF

Judith Steele recounts in hard words the stations of a life, from childhood through senile dementia. She finishes it in a town like Darwin, in a fanfare of birds and butterflie, redeeming the waste lands the collection begins with. This is not vaporous poetry. Steele strikes flint. Sparks fly.

– Douglas Spangle, Stuart H. Holbrook Literary Award recipient, poet, translator, author, *A White Concrete Day*

For Australian poet Judith Steele, not only the world of dreams but also the world of childhood is a great inspiration. Her poetry collection *Islands of Disbelief* draws from nature and myths. Her view of old age is unsentimentally precise. Nevertheless, confidence and a true zest for life permeate her verses: "Some grace drops into my dreams / between dreary islands of disbelief."

– Florian Vetsch, poet, essayist, translator, author, *The Fire Potions, Tanger Trance,* and *43 New Poems*

Magpies patrol the grass, and doves
call from somewhere in the distance,
and it seems as if such lucky days in
a country still lucky for some,
will break my heart.

She says she must be careful because her friend was found dead. She says she must be careful because some men make snuff movies.

Reprobate / GobQ Books, Portland, Oregon 2022

iSLANDS F DiSBELiEF

ISBN 978-1-64871-465-8

$ 15.00

All rights reserved. No part of this book may be reproduced in any form without written permission of the copyright owners.

The images in this book have been reproduced with knowledge & prior consent of the artists concerned, & no responsibility is accepted by the producer, publisher, or printer for any infringement of copyright or otherwise, arising from the contents of this publication. Every effort has been made to ensure that credits accurately comply with information supplied. We apologize for any inaccuracies that may have occurred & will resolve inaccurate or missing information in any subsequent reprinting of the book.

10 9 8 7 6 5 4 3 2

||| Cover & Interior Design: T. Warburton y Bajo ||| Int. red star youth images: T. Warburton y Bajo |||

These or earlier versions of these poems have appeared in:

Coastlines
Dymocks Northern Territory Literary Awards
Five Bells
Gobshite Quarterly
In Other Words Merida (webzine)
Northern Perspective
Plum Tree Tavern (webzine)
Tema (Zagreb) (translation)
The Animist (webzine)
Thylazine (webzine)
Tinta D (translation) (webzine)
Yellow Moon

Table of Contents

Bushfire Dreaming	15
Never	16
My Grandfather	17
The Child Remembers	18
Neverland	20
Rose Undaughter	22
Reflections	25
Waterbed	27
Sorry	28
Never Again	29
Gone	31
Quiet	32
Suburban Idyll	33
Diurnal	34
Night Lights	35
Trees	37
Duty One	39
An Aspect of Chronic Fatigue Syndrome with Tropical Light	42
The Walls Around Australia	43
Chairman, Community Housing	44
The News	45
Bilateral Fractures	47
Ode To My Feet	48

Oh, Ageing!	50
To Peg, 1944-2002	51
Genetic Longevity	52
Dementia Games	53
Duty Two	57
A Bird in the Hand	59
Dementia Fears	60
Seapath	62
In The Stocks	63
Bemos	65
Water Sister	68
Sky Driving	90
Sea Tribe	91
On This Summer Day (untitled)	93

Index of Titles	96
Index of First Lines	98
Author Bio	100

BUSHFIRE DREAMING

The bush burns, animals burn, houses burn,
    sky burns
In the sky a crimson koala burns
Now the sky is burning black
The sky is soot
Falls on our faces.
Now a whirling in the wind, whirling of
    feathers,
demonic whirling as if the devil is in it
It is crows, a cry of crows, whirling on their
    wings,
They land in the trees, not to rest
They hang from trees black and burned
dripping with blood, dripping red rain on us
as we try to find air.

NEVER

I am 10 years old. It is my mother's 30th birthday. I am going to school. I have left the house, left my mother standing at the back door, waving. She is happy for once. She has on a blue and white checked cotton dress. I walk to the front, out the gate, along past the bright green of the local football oval and towards the marshy creek where we children go at weekends to catch tadpoles. Today I turn the corner to walk to the tram-stop. The sky is pale blue, the air on my skin is dry. I am wearing a cotton frock and carrying a school-case with my initials on it. I know who lives in all these houses. I am going past a house that has a low stone fence, pink and purple flowers, a house like ours with a frontage of pale blocks of limestone. I walk swiftly, full of energy and awareness. I feel the outlines of myself very clearly and my spirit is singing. I am an utterly different person from my mother. I am not her. She is 30. But I am 10, and I will never be 30.

MY GRANDFATHER

My grandfather rocked me wrapped securely
in his arms, up and down the shadowed
    passageway,
singing his forever song
Tooralay Ooralay Addiddie.

My grandfather made the shining path
of stones: glittering quartz and mica rolled
by his strong arms and giant concrete wheel,
to carpets of security.

My grandfather built a magic house
of beans, cool green inside to hide and eat,
crusader's tent for dreaming worlds
of giant-killing feats.

My grandfather climbed the giant's tower
at Osborne. My grandfather made the sun.
He brought it home each day to where I'd
    wait
by the big white gate.

My grandfather died. They said.
They cried.
But I am a stone, a sharp white stone.
I stand and wait by the big white gate.

THE CHILD REMEMBERS

She was warm in the water   splashing
& sliding   her small white body
could swim   in the big white bath
and her grandfather brought the big white
    towel
to wrap her in
she was warm with love and joy
as she ran to the dark front room
and stood by the fire to be dried.

There were shadows in the room
her grandmother's brown, very tight around
    her
the mother's faint blue was hunched to grey
the white light of her grandfather stayed
    behind her.

Before her a new sharp shape:
"This is your father, home from the war."
He looked at her, and looked at her.
she stood still   chilled.
She suddenly knew   it was all her fault
everything   everything
in the world.

*I can still see that fire
the orange gladiolus
burning in the corner of my eye.*

NEVERLAND

As a child she followed Cuchulain
through Arthur Mee's Encyclopaedia,
was sure she would go to Ireland
and step through veils to Tir na N'ogh,
be safe from ridicule in emerald green vales
of the land of shadow.

On the four-sided seats made for school-
    children
on the perimeters of slippery olive-stained
    asphalt,
she told stories, every lunchtime, of the Little
    Hound,
and Hermes Zeus Poseidon Dis, and from
    Italy, Ginevra hiding
in the chest she closed mischievously, her
    bones found years later
in the lace of the wedding dress. Sometimes
    she changed the endings,
allowed Ginevra to be found, to marry, safe in
    the land of story.

At High School, story-telling history teachers
taught her to barrack for Athens not Sparta,
Greece, not Rome or Persia.
Oh yes she would go to Ireland, Greece,
    Rome.

She knew no stories about her own land
except those told by dots, dashes and arrows
of different colours on the map of Australia.
She had no interest in explorers, always wondered
how they could discover something already there.

Once, at a Church social, there were brown children
from the orphanage. Someone said their parents were dead,
then that their mothers didn't want them. She knew
there was something there not explained, not said,
some gap she couldn't patch with a web of story.

She married. Silence. No story that fits
with her other stories, unless it were the mystery
of brown children in orphanages. Or perhaps
Cuchulian bound to a rock, Ginevra suffocated.
In any case, she never went to Ireland.

ROSE UNDAUGHTER

My daughter was a rose a rose
who grew inside me
thorns
to prick my conscience. Did you
did you? Are you are you?
Yes oh yes.
The water in the shower it pricks
like thorns the swollen breast.

My daughter was a thorn a thorn
in my parents' flesh
sharper than a serpent's tooth.
Who oh who?
I will not say his name not his
not he with rose curved lips.

My daughter was the blankness
of the space inside me
in the convent;
stairs I climbed, meals I cooked,
lies I told, the adolescent laughter
and the tears that others cried at night
not me not me not yet.

My daughter was the black lonely night,
the hissed hatred of the nurse's
Serves You Right!
They pierced my breasts with thorns
and bound my signing hand with silence.
Still I wept
and so they let me see her.

My daughter was a rose a rose
her white rose face her lips like his
my child with rose curved lips.

My daughter was the child who screamed
inside the locked-up room of dreams
who beat her fists against the doors
and ran through echoing corridors
of night between the days
and years of nonexistence.

My daughter was a rose a rose
a white rose in my diary
the day I wrote to find her.

My daughter is a rose a rose
a Frida Kahlo deep red rose.
A flower of life her life her own
with thorns she grows and wields
with wit
and thorns inborn she bears
with gallantry and humour.
My spicy rose undaughter.

REFLECTIONS

Shadows
In the new house
the mother faints
frequently
The child bends over her
puzzled by the mother's faint smile
Does she see, even then
the martyr's grin?

Twenty years later
the child's baby
strokes blue bruises
on his mother's face.
She will never forget his soft hands,
his puzzled frown.

Again
The mother and child in the house,
the father gone to work.
Watch me dance, says the child
again and again
Again and again the mother applauds
against her screaming boredom.

Play with my cars, says the child's child
in the high chair, on the floor
and outside in the dust
Again and again
the mother says vroom vroom vroom
Again! says the child.

Waiting
The child plays the mother's games
hoping her mother will look at her
instead of the faint distance
through the laundry window.

The adult child, scrubbing nappies
looks into the distance
Are you coming, Are you coming
Knights of Camelot?

WATERBED

Mirror, stained glass window, curtains
throw light and shadow on the red quilt,
undulating centre surrounded by still life

How long do you think this will last?
It's not your bed

Life on the ocean wave
lasts only until the night
he sleeps elsewhere

and you attack his bed
with a carving knife

Early hours of morning weeping
you try to patch the waterbed
with masking tape

He comes home
The wounds are fatal.

SORRY

I was reading a poem
about a mother's memory
of her son's first schoolday,
and I remembered first day
for both of us
at the new secondary school.

From the staff-room window
I saw my son standing alone,
hands in pockets
of his new grey pants,
slouched sufficiently to suggest
to schoolyard observers his ease
and approachability

but I saw
his chin tilted
eyes straight
shoulders squared

against whatever battering
I'd dragged him to
this time

his spirit as always
sternly alert
and courageous.

NEVER AGAIN

Another Anzac Day
to remember what?
My father's anger? Drunkenness
on the few Anzac Days
he celebrated with his mates?
My mother's grim righteousness?
My father's *War is Hell
and I won't talk about it?*
If you had talked, I might have understood.

When I delivered pamphlets
for the Vietnam Moratoruim
you shouted at me because you fought
    "them."
No you didn't I said.
They're all the same
you said. *War is Hell*, you said.
Yes, Dad, that's why I'm marching
against this one!

War is Hell, my mother's father also said
after Gallipoli, The Somme. He wouldn't talk
either. A good man, my father too,
so many good men, so much better
if they all talked. But I understand
they wanted to forget, not remember.

But when I was a child it seemed to me they
    were always talking,
in the manner of *I didn't go through the war
    for this*
and *If you'd gone through the depression you'd
    eat up your food*
and *We went through the depression and
    the war,
but you don't know anything.* No I don't,
because you won't tell me, but are always
    angry
with children who can't know what you
    won't say.

I am writing this eight years after your
    death, Dad,
when your grandson and his children
    honour you
better than I did, knowing more than we
    did.

When massed flags fly may they also
    remember
that you said: *War is Hell.*

GONE

The quietest moment that I can remember
was the moment after my father stopped
    breathing
in the small room in the hospital,
the small room for dying.

My son sat on one side of my father
I sat on the other.
I was telling my son the story
of how, as a child, I had a pet galah
but didn't really want it –
I couldn't stand it being caged.
And one day I left the cage door open
just a bit. In the morning it was gone.

It was the moment after I stopped speaking
that my father stopped breathing

QUIET

Earth is buried
beneath faded leaves,
shades of autumn
fallen on winter

Today no rain no wind
no sun, only sounds
of silence, dead cold,
the taste of regret.

Magpies foraging
on the baseball oval
have no songs

Grey and still,
the Patawalonga Creek.

SUBURBAN IDYLL

In the street today, there's a kind of music
that breaks the morning silence with the
    single notes
of a gullwing, a butterfly, a child's amazed
    eyes.

Birds fly soprano in the afternoon symphonies
weaved by trees; a spiralling trumpet blown
by a firehawk, a flute piped by a dragonfly.

A thin Chinese paint-brush
Tips the evening trees with apricot light,
scribbles silk dragons on the sky.

The sea chants a mauve lullaby.

DIURNAL

Circling and recircling
their alloted streets and suburbs
the adolescent couriers
on their bicycles
delivering.

Hovering and watching
doors of their neighbours
like young hunting hawks
waiting to swoop
devouring.

Turning and returning
whistling a warning
to their consignors
whose hands are held out
falconing.

NIGHT LIGHTS

Insomniac wired to a Walkman,
I doze one-eared through music and bad news

wake one morning to hear two sex workers
being interviewed: one works in Australia,
only visits women, and says he feels safe
because the Agency knows where he is
with his coloured flavoured condoms,
and his suit he wears for the good hotels
He doesn't need the job
but he likes the extra money
and he wouldn't tell his parents
No.

And then there's a woman who's standing on a street
and yes her parents know what she does –
they look after her son in Soweto –
and she says she will die
if her son ever knows ...
She says she must be careful
because some men won't wear condoms
She says she must be careful
because her friend was found dead
She says she must be careful

because some men make snuff movies
and I see lives blown by the world's winds
and snuffed unsung by a human obscenity
which desires darkness, and finds the
    snuffing of a light
the ultimate ecstacy.

TREES

Indian laburnum
drops petals in Darwin streets
I remember at the bus-stop
golden flowers galore
scattered sunlight at my feet.

Hans Heysen's Trees

1.
Heysen paints gum trees
so solidly white
I want to peel strips of bark
and drop them on the shining floor
of the Gallery.

2.
Trees stand in a group
for the moment,
hold their breath
for the observer.
When the painter leaves
they'll stump away
find another fine place
to stand together.

Ficus Albipilia

Let me rest in your roots
Hide in your alcoves
Close your doors on me
Let me grow to tree

DUTY ONE

Bad Girl Says

She's a vampire.
She's eaten all the freedom
from her children's souls
and now dives in
with her honeyed lies
and whining repetitions
of devotion, to the blood
of grandchildren. Blood
is what she needs and gets
and MINE she says
of great-grandchildren,
and every child sister brother other
she manipulates with vicious whispers
of invented or twisted scandal,
plain lies, or truth in backstabbing secrets,
till they surrender to silence,
while she goes on
undying, invincible, unending denial
in her blood-drenched smile.

Madwoman Says

Run, run as fast as you can,
you can't catch me I'm the non-admitter
of anything. I don't even admit I'm running,
running on the spot, on mother's treadmill,
    running
to her tune, whipped by her martrydom, her
    delusions,
her refusal to admit her actions words malice
    scandal lies and guilt,
her plotting and sneaking gollumnature, her
    precious precious vampire self.

Sad Person Says

She closes her eyes
to signal to me
she has closed her ears
and won't hear my words
(as usual) I wonder
when she closes her eyes forever
will I still try to tell her
what she will not hear?

*

Boredom is going about someone else's
 business
too often, and for too long, and for no good
 reason.

AN ASPECT OF CHRONIC FATIGUE SYNDROME WITH TROPICAL LIGHT

Once beloved emerald light
I've overeaten you
too often swum in dense green suns
now light eats me
fades my substance, wanes my mind.

And I am tired and tired and tired and tired and

language has left me
packed its paraphernalia,
slipped down cryptic corridors of time
to changing borderlines
of fossil memory

Still beloved emerald god,
you melt my brain
and eat my flesh,
corrode my bones

Mutate me.

Let me fall through your coruscations,
slip between solidities, drift dissolving.
Let your light eat me.

THE WALLS AROUND AUSTRALIA

are long grey waves
rolling continuously
over untold stories, deaths unlamented,
unceremonious sea burials
of excised truth.

The walls within the mind
are shadowed backdrops
for phantom fears re-conjured
by dalangs who've discarded all the voices
except the monotonal chorus of some scripted
    lines
re-drawn in shifting sands.

The walls inside Australia
wail with echoes
of convicts flogged, the stolen ones,
the silent scream of stitched-up lips, last cries
of our grandchildren's children drowning
anonymously

beneath the walls around Australia.

CHAIRMAN, COMMUNITY HOUSING

In case there was to be an event
that might in future
be of significance
to the motions on notice,
I factored in situations
from my downloaded thoughts,
had pre-discussions with myself
and present you
with your consensus.

THE NEWS

In the year 2020 the media ceased reporting wars

since fatigues were the customary dress of everywhere

and boundaries overflown by interlocking movements

of guerillas and militias and feral police and military

combining and splitting and drawing new boundaries

ceaselessly, it became more daring to report in areas

of temporary agreement, but after a while, the militias

photographing the media to accuse them of atrocities

the militias themselves were about to commit, and the

guerillas photographing militia and police, the military

taking over communications, and reporting victory

till the guerillas outreported them, eventually, no-one

could remember who currently controlled the media

where, or even which side was talking, and the children

born of the fighters had only the haziest idea of where

their parents came from originally, and so they made

new alliances, but that too is already history's history.

BILATERAL FRACTURES

My hands unhandily wrapped
by plaster handcuffs
At the airport X-Ray I explain
I need to carry on this piece of metal
bent twice to form a flexible rod
so plastered hands can hold one end,
on the other end a lump of plastic
to wrap with loo paper.
It's not a weapon, I say, it's … um …
Go through! says the woman at the airport
      X-Ray

Two years later

My strong crooked wrists work
like old tools one can't replace
They can dance ungracefully

There are things they can't do
some buttons, taps, tops, knobs
some yoga has become impossible.

I never returned the bottom-wiper
to the hospital – you never know
what you might need again.

ODE TO MY FEET

Once my feet could twinkle in toe-shoes,
leap from the ground and stretch in mid-air
Now they wouldn't dare.
But still they take me
to where we're going.

Once my feet were often bare
On beaches, on grass, or just
in the house, in tropical air.
Now always stuffed
inside socks, waking or sleeping,
in cold air they hate. But still
they go on, to wherever we're going.

Once I strutted on stilettos
Now my feet and I love comfort.
Once I painted my toenails
Now they're white claws.

Once my feet never stumbled
Now they throw me to the ground.
But still they stand me up again
and take me where we're going.

We know where we're going
is into the last fall, the end
of standing up again, but still,
we'll go there together
forever.

OH, AGEING!

OH evolution, why not devise a mechanism
for sudden death? before the body
crumbles and fails and cancerises and
dries, before the bones shrink and the
teeth fall out, the muscles waste and the
skin flab hangs, before more than words
slip from the brain, before confusion
and absent-mindedness turn to fear and
madness and hopeless dependence.
OH evolution I suppose you arranged that to
resign us to death. Even to hope for it?
OH evolution, try again!

TO PEG, 1944–2002

I was expecting her husband
to answer the phone
& say she was still
in hospital
or something worse.
But she answered herself
in her usual cheerful voice
and my heart leapt with joy.
Then she told me
that she – a workaholic –
had left work
and was writing
her Will.

Afterwards
I walk the night
always followed
by a grinning moon.

GENETIC LONGEVITY

When all the older males of the family are dead
And all the old women keep living
with stents in their arteries, pain in their bodies,
malice and trivia on their minds

After all the strokes they've partly recovered from
with narrowing and muffling of the brain
After I've repeated the same answers
to the same questions
time out of someone's mind.

After one day at a poetry workshop
I find I can only write of trivia
and malice

Then rumours of the advent
of my own dementia
whisper in my blood.

DEMENTIA GAMES

1.

She never raises her voice
Her anger is expressed
by the wheels of her walker
veering into the paths
of other pedestrians,
or by ramming their heels
with her wheels,
and always running over
my sandalled toes
again and again.

2.

Could you get your appointments on the same
day?
I ask her.
It would save me coming every day

She looks away from me
her bottom lip sticks out
like a 2-year-old
contemplating tantrum.

Don't you just love it
when they do that?
my hairdresser exclaims.

Her father when he got undressed
left his clothes on the floor
She picked up, washed, ironed, folded,
and showed him where they were.

He phoned her brother, said
She always takes my clothes away.

3.

A well-dressed woman
weekly discussed poetry
in my friend's bookshop.
One day she bought twenty books

Her family phoned him and said
How Could You? She Has Dementia!

He said, But,
How Could I Know?
She has always seemed
So knowledgeable.

Yes, they said,
That is Her Act.

4.

And on the one hand
I think we all put on an Act
most of the time

And on the other
I have seen my mother's Act –
so smiley and brave with neighbours
Poor old lady they think,
Those dreadful daughters!

And my aunt's Act –
condescension
to people privileged
to attend to her

(my husband
so jolly and friendly
no-one could believe
he bashed me every night)

And so I think
my mother's and my aunt's Acts
are lifetime attitudes
solidified by age,

all that is left
when the rest has gone.

Oh but why do I fear
what Act of mine
will be my all?

DUTY TWO

Stuck in mud in fog in anger
Stuck in sensible. Throw it away.
Give it to mother.
Stuck in stupid
self-imprisonment
Fenced with dense palings
pale jail of paralysis.

DUTY THREE

Yet
I'm sorry for her sometimes
So I am held.

And held
by the times I failed my son,
and his mercy after long anger.
By my once and always failure
to support my birth-daughter,
in any way whatsoever,
and her unpunishing.

And held
by my sisters,
sweet and bitterness

And by memory of my father
going to work, ill and well,
again and again and again.

I am held.
Stet.

A BIRD IN THE HAND

I listen to Judith Wright's poetry about birds
read by her daughter on radio
for forty-five whole minutes
and for forty-five minutes
my soul is whole

except for the the knowledge
that even if I can't write like that
I could write something
write now
instead of acceding to the bleak prospects of
duty

as if there would be a day when duty's done
as if then I could write.

There will be a day
when it's all done,
but it won't be a day
for writing.

DEMENTIA FEARS

Now I've seen different dementias, the woman who hates children, smiling women, sad men, moaning women, men angry, women agitated, the woman who likes to show her pants, frightened women like my aunt, nasty men or women, oh they talk about elder abuse, but I could tell you stories about abusive elders. Then there was the woman at Uniting Care Christmas Day party table with tears running down her cheeks, eating a sausage roll with tears, eating a cupcake with tears, a good looking woman not so much older than me.

I remember my forgettings and confusions, wonder if I will end wandering slowly in the shadows of the past, better that perhaps than struggling through the shallows of all I can manage of the present. The past comes into the light, the present fades, then memory ebbs to a sea of silence.

Better a dash to the end, a dive into the deep, on a day when I know what I'm doing.

Unknowing is what I fear. Not knowing I am
wearing dirty clothes, have unwashed hair.
How lightning the line between knowing and
not, how unknowing one may cross the line as
the time to go slips by, and going is not made
easy, and suddenly one forgets one meant to go,
adapts to life with a bib and waterproof pants.

Are they worse than days of undirection on
the threshold of darkness, the degradations the
injured brain inflicts on the body?

What are my genes? On my mother's side, long
lived physical toughness and mental decline;
on my father's, physical decline with the mind
unimpaired, earlier death. Which genes do I
gamble on? I say I will go willing into that good
night, but at the time, how does one go? And
how know the time?

It must be now. It must always be now.

SEAPATH

As the earth turns
I watch the sun
spread gold-dust on the sea
For a moment the guitar sings
again by firelight
A child's eyes shine
without disappointment

My eyes look for yours
in the face of a stranger
as if I could find you again
and myself

Once I was lightly sure
of my path
Now I am heavy with regret

The people I could have been multiply
as I subtract what I am not

the future unlikely
to bring addition

I take off my shoes
and walk to the sun
only in dreams.

IN THE STOCKS

on the pyre on the cross on the bonfire, witch. Burn baby burn o Kali who brings darkness into the light. How they appropriate you, Christians who call themselves progressives, borrowing your attributes to give to Christ, and not acknowledging where they found them, borrowing Tagore's poetry and giving it to Christians, and not acknowledging the author, but that's Christianity the habitual borrower, the great adaptor, that's the way to everlasting life.

Christianity, you burned me as a witch more than once; first when I was adolescent and the priest who kissed me when I got pregnant once, said, when I got pregnant twice, I thought you were a good girl who made one mistake, but you're not, are you! No. Good enough for an adult married priest to kiss in the car after baby-sitting his kids though. Not good enough to risk forgiving twice. Wise of you. Good means Clever? Is that what God means too?

I left you, Christianity, and then returned, only to be burned again, for my adultery, it seems, and yet my accuser was my most determined seducer. But what does that matter to you, Christianity? Did you look for Mary Magdalen's partners? Did you see what made her what she was? She was healed by Christ, not by Christianity, so Established, so Exclusive.

I thought you were a good girl who made one mistake, but you're not, are you! No, I am a stupid girl who cannot learn from her mistakes, who does not know what is the lesson, who was long ago taught to look away, look away, when anybody hurt her. My teacher was a lay preacher, what a rhyme, what a stereotype hypocrite. But that's life, if it didn't happen so often, it wouldn't so often be said.

In the stocks. Throw your rotten eggs and words at me. You tempted me, Christianity, twice, then threw me away. Will I be tempted thrice? You are right, there IS something about me that needs correcting. Only, I can't correct it. Once bitten, I'm thrice ready to be bitten again.

BEMOS

When I first went to Kupang, West Timor, in 1989, my ears felt assaulted by continual beep-beeps of small passenger vans known as bemos, the shouts of their konjaks (conductors), as they leant out of the doors yelling destinations, along with encouragement to pedestrians who could wave them down from anywhere on the road, while pop, rock or Timorese folk music blared from speakers mounted on the multi-coloured and decorated bemos. Their names were emblazoned on the side: Sinar Mas (ray of gold), Body Rock, Optimis, Elvis, Sweetheart, Pahlawan (hero).

On later visits when I learned to use them, I found them the most convenient form of public transport possible, so many, so often, going to so many places. I got used to squashing into a space on one of the two narrow benches of passenger seating. Sometimes someone would call out a warning orang barat (westerner) and everyone would shift up for a person fatter than Timorese; some would smile, others scowl and mutter. There might be men holding groomed fighting cocks on their laps, women with multiple bags of shopping, and always there was the smell of clove cigarettes.

The konjaks soon got to know who lived where, and sometimes seemed determined to pick me up and take me there, even when I was walking to somewhere else, or to grab my bags in the market and put them into the bemo that was my usual destination, even if I hadn't finished shopping.

Once I stayed at a hotel further out from the town than usual, on the road to the port. I found it very hard to get a bemo here because the drivers wanted to pick up or deliver people from inter-island ferries, not to waste time with someone going halfway and paying less. Like the locals, I could stand on the road and say Aduh! (oh my!) while the bemos whizzed by, or else just give up and walk, a long way. Sometimes one or more of us could get a ride on the water-truck. And once a Bugis fisherman came up from the beach and said: "Ibu, if you are going to Australia I can take you on my boat. Don't worry, I know the way!"

Whenever I go back to Australia, the bemos are what I miss most. How silent the streets of Darwin seem. How I long to be back, where the bemos screech and flash and sing, where the konjak calls ke mana?(where are you going?). I'm too sexy for my hat, sing the bemos, Oh my love my darling, sing the bemos, sopir baik-hati (a good-hearted driver) call the bemos. Mari! (Let's go!) says the konjak, gathering up my bags, and I must go, whether I will or no, and we go. To Oekabiti, Baumata, Camplong, Kupang Kupang Kupang, hey you coming missus? Yes!

WATER SISTER

Silau (Indonesian):
dazzled, temporarily blinded by the glare

dramatis personae

Silau – an island in Indonesia
Kate – an Australian tourist
Jonni – a local businessman, hustler
Pira – a woman of Silau
Kiras – Pira's husband

WATER SISTER

I was the last virgin sacrificed to the crocodile god
by the Sea Prince, my brother – the only man
who knew I was no virgin. In his memory
I drowned all men of Silau who disturbed me

and pale men who came in boats
bigger than the Raja's house, and some
who walked into the sea to curse me,
or bless me, or because they desired me.

The women sing at the edge of the sea
that I am quiet now, desire only the sun.
Yet sometimes a woman comes alone
and whispers to me. Fishermen still fear me.

More boats, more people, dark and pale,
come all the time, some of them women
who swim with me, knowingly or not.
Here is one, dazzled by our butterflies
and blinded by herself.

KATE

Butterflies above the sea
brush yellow wings against my skin

before unveiling the island's white smile of sand
beneath a steep brown hill
fringed and crowned with coconut and lontar
palm.

I leap from the tourist boat
into that green sea

A story-book island
I want to hear a story.

KATE AND JONNI

You like Silau, Kate?
I hope to develop it
as a tourist resort
What is your opinion?

I say I don't know.
I think Iwant it
for myself.

I have to go back this afternoon, Kate
to catch the plane to Jakarta
This is the room I stay in when I'm here.
Come in with me.

KATE IN JONNI'S ROOM

I do as he desires.

In any Paradise
I am compliantly guilty.

In Jakarta I was a little in love
with his wide smile and hooting laugh,
his competence. But this is not Jakarta.

PIRA

The one with red hair goes with Jonni
She can go with whoever she likes
And he can go, back and forth, to Java and Bali
and all the islands
making money, changing the islands
to suit tourists.

Now he has his eyes on Silau.
and he paid me well
to find out who will sell.

I know already
but I take the money.
He's my cousin's cousin
and through him there will be a future
for me and Kidas and our children.

KATE STAYS

Jonni leaves,
tells Kidas the boatman
to take care of me.
Kidas leads me to a palm-thatched hut,
says This is your house.

PIRA

This is your house you didn't build,
and this is your meal you didn't cook
These are your beans you didn't grow,
your fish you didn't catch.
This is your house you don't have to clean
and that is my husband who smiles at you.

We are the people to look after you,
to smile at you, be nice to you.

Like a child you have nothing to do but play
because you can pay

KATE

KATE: NIGHT AND DAY

In my palm roofed hut last night
I saw a giant warrior with a keris
He stamped your sand beneath his elegant feet.
Above him, a skeleton
tangled in vines
hanging from a tree.

I accepted that dream, or vision
as part of your story, Silau.

At dawn I walk pink sands,
slim moon held in salt mist.

I glide into your water
swim noiselessly
it is you, Silau
who whisper Stay to me.

In the afternoon I climb the hill
to women washing clothes in spring water
rising from white stone, and stones again,
circling stones, stained with blood
(I think) or maybe betel juice.

Behind the stones, dark trees and vines
remind me of my dream, and suddenly
I fear the skeleton.

I turn away quickly, stumble
into dead ends in the village
Polite words, closed faces of women
direct me back to the beach.
In the evening I play billiards with Kidas.
He sings a song
in Silau's liquid language

His scarred eyelid droops
over a glittering eye
He whistles now
Island In the Sun

All my days, Kidas,
I could live here.
But he asks me
Where is your house,
your husband? In Australia?

He says he also is unmarried
Unlikely, in this culture.
But he has said it.

KATE: SUN AND MOON

After a storm, the sky pales from indigo to green,
leaks into the sea.
I swim far out, tread water,
float in an emerald world.

The sun pierces me.
Sea whispers of coolness.
I slide within

bear sun's captured light
to gold of sand beneath the sea.

The sun and I leap
with green waves
ride them to the shore

Beached
on the last throes of sunset

Alone again
I watch a swollen red moon
heave itself over the horizon

watch Kidas guide his boat home
by moon's lurid light,
walk to me out of the sea
Come, Kate, with me.

KATE: YOUR SUN HAS WINGS

Next day, he takes me out to dive the reef
and shows me butterflies again
He says they are wings of the sun
come down to tease the Water Sister
below the sea.

She was a woman of Silau,
virgin sacrificed to the crocodile god
in the days of the Raja.
Her spirit searches for someone
to stay with her.

Even the sun she tries to capture, see –
now she has his light beneath the sea.
But she can never keep him.
He escapes on the butterflies' wings.

KATE: YOUR MOON DRIPS HONEY

After sunset
Kidas comes to the beach
puts his hand through my arm
He sings, softly, his tongue of the sea

Lost in the wave, my resolution
not to sleep with you again, drowned
in the green swell of Silau's sea

Melted in your breath, matahariku,
my questions about your marriage
What can I do but whisper with you
Selalu. Always.

In my hut we fall into a dizzy kiss,
float in fallen stars, and I'm not forty
but fourteen, with my first love
Paradise regained.

KATE: STONE GAME, FISH GAME

At the spring I play knucklebones
with two schoolgirls, using stones
one two, one two three.
Women walk to the restaurant
with baskets of fruit and vegetables
Their lips and teeth are smeared with betel-
juice.
Is one of them his wife?
One two three.

Evening, on the beach, children dig in wet sand,
scoop up stranded baitfish.
One boy digs a channel, makes a river
for one little fish to swim
in temporary freedom.

KIDAS AND KATE: STORIES

Kidas tells me
about the Water Sister and the sun,
about rajas and sailors and war,
and the pilots who fell from the sky
and died in their parachutes
in Silau's trees.

He tells me to be careful of magic
on Silau, and that he can protect me.

But he doesn't believe
I live from job to job,
hand to hand, will go home
with no money. He throws back his head
and laughs. How cunning a liar I am!

If I can go to Australia,
he smiles at me
I will be rich.

I will catch bait-fish on Silau, I say
You will teach English in Darwin.
We laugh.
The villagers watch us.

PIRA WAITS

You won't be rich in Australia, Kidas,
but on Silau, when Jonni returns
and builds his hotel. I will cook
and you will work for Jonni
although you hate him.

Get rid of your dreams and pretence
with this pink woman, a soft melon.
I will tell you what to do, as I have
since we were children.

BROKEN IS MORNING

Dammed rivers
children dig in the sand
trap high tide baitfish

Crimson streams
float on the sea
behind dugout canoes
of fishermen
spitting betel juice

Dynamite
cracks the morning
Villagers flow down the hill
stare at commercial fishing boats

Silence their children.

Indonesia! says Kidas
And spits into the sand.

JONNI'S PLANS

Next day a crowded tourist boat.
Someone waves. It's Jonni.

In Jonni's room Kate evades questions
about returning to Jakarta or Australia,
ask him about his plans. He says he is here
to sign papers with landowners
who will sell their land
for his resort.

JONNI: PLENTY OF ISLANDS

There are plenty of other islands
he said as he told her his plans
for building the concrete units
moving the stones from the sand.

An island boy himself
grown sleek on the tourist streets
of the capital – time to live closer to home.

What about your island, then? she asked
He laughed. There are plenty of other islands.

JONNI: PLENTY OF TOURISTS

Just be quiet Kate and listen to me
You like this island. You can stay here
later, for nothing, in my new place I will build,
and you will tell your friends in Australia
to come here for holidays, instead of Bali.

You do not want to? You do not want me
any more, perhaps? Indeed.
There are plenty of other tourists
who will be happy to do it,
plenty of women too

Plenty of women like Kate,
wanting a slice of paradise.

She goes back to the larger island with Jonni,
but just to go to shops. They are polite
to one another. She misses the joker of Jakarta

but supposes that's the man
who wants to make a joke of Silau.

GOOD LUCK

Kate returns to Silau in the village boat,
crowded with bags of rice,
children with sticky lollies, men who grin,

women who mutter.
As they come closer to Silau, water is sunset
silver and suddenly
silver dolphins leap before the bow. Kidas turns
from the tiller
and laughs at Kate. Bahagia, he says, Good
Luck.

KIDAS: MAYBE

Kate says she wants to stay on Silau
but she buys clothes and books
we can't afford. We work in the gardens
to grow just enough corn to eat
and sell the rest for rice.

This is my home. It was my ancestor's home
before the Dutch came, and before the
Indonesians
renamed it Silau. In our language it was the
centre
but now it is only on the edge
of Indonesia. Now they are coming,
the ones with big plans.

Our fish will be caught
by the big boats now, and sold in Jakarta.

I will help build Jonni's hotel,
fetch and carry, bend my head to him.
This is what Pira wants.

But if I can get more money somewhere else
I won't have to work for Jonni.
I can come back and start my own business
with a glass-bottom boat. Later. After Australia.
I can have two homes. Kate and Pira,
two wives.

KATE: MAYBE

Good luck, he said, and again my heart
believed him. And I believe Silau gave me
dolphins and butterflies, visions and stories
to tell me I belong here.

Yet Kidas
wants me to leave, and help him leave too.
Would he ask me that if he was married?
Maybe it's true that he has no wife?
So then why not? Why not help him
and see what happens?

If I did that, could we come back?
Could we have two homes?
Is it true?

KIDAS AND KATE: THE END OF STORIES

WIFE

This night, Kidas says, I will show you
what you saw in your dreams
Indeed there were pilots fell in the war
but more, on Silau there are powers
that send enemies into certain trees. But do not worry
if you are with me. I can get you down. He laughs.

We walk to the spring, turn away, skirt the circling stones
into sharp-leaved bushes he holds apart for me
The evening is breathless with close crowded vine wreathed trees,
black trees I remember from my waking dream.

Kidas is shadowed. His scarred eye glitters
as he whispers Look there!
No! I want to leave it as a dream,
not to see the skeleton.
Another voice shrieks behind me

You dare bring her here!

I turn. She looks at me with a mocking smile,
triumphant and young, a slim gold woman
Your wife, Kidas?
He looks confused, like a guilty boy.
And this place stinks of decay.

I push back through the bushes
Whore! sneers the wife.
I run down to my hut, lock the door
so Kidas cannot come to me
this night.

KATE: THE END OF STORIES

WHORE

Sleepless and dreamless, I doze in the morning,
wake to a world leached of magic. So once I dreamed
of a warrior crushing Silau, and a skeleton in a tree
and thought the spirits of the island favoured me
with secrets. I should have known I hanged that spectre of myself, the whore,
and Kidas won't get me down from that tree.

As for the warrior with the knife –
Jonni – slicing the sand into strips of resorts.
All the tourists to come are a mirror for me,
who wanted only the paradise I saw, not the reality.

And in this tourist hut, the marked old mirror
reflects my smoker's lined mouth and mottled skin.

KATE'S LAST SWIM

The sea was dull grey
Small waves crawled onto the shore,
sank into trampled sand.

I took my snorkel and mask
away from the safety of the beach
stumbled over limestone rock,
scratched my body from legs to chest.
I saw death through my mask
Sea-snake, Stonefish, Stingray

Hold out your hand, put down your foot,
if you want to stay with me.
Picked clean your bones will gleam
with the light inside my sea.

Three chances at death Silau offered me,
and all of them
my dull cowardice refused.

WIFE AND HUSBAND

PIRA

Poor man
you wanted her freedom
Her freedom was only
to be alone

KIDAS

She dreamed to stay
I dreamed to go
She goes. I stay.
Now it is time
for Pira's dream
Unless ....

WATER SISTER

I was the last woman sacrificed to the
crocodile god
Any whore can swim with me
especially one who hears my voice so clearly.

I offered you your wish, to stay with me.
Why did you go, shamefaced?
That was man's magic, the place of death
and skeletons, where my brother took me.

Death with me
is rid of the heavy flesh, not hanging in a tree
but surfing the moonlight waves,
eating the daylight sun

The women sing at the edge of the sea
that I am quiet now.
Fishermen still fear me.

But you swam well with me,
your red hair waving

You could have stayed
and caught your fisherman
to share with me.

More boats, more people, dark and pale
come all the time.

There will be others
dazzled by my butterflies.

SKY DRIVING

Early southern winter, morning northern sky
seals the bowl of itself intensely blue,
as if to remind ceramicists
where they first found that colour.

Late afternoon, sky to the south
gathers smoky grey clouds,
herds them on the horizon,
allows pale blue to float above.

Westwards over the water, pale blue prevails.
In early evening, yellow streaks of sunsetting
recline on darkening sea.

Eastwards the curves of hills
are glowing purple. Above them,
reflecting their lines and tints,
long waves of violet clouds.

Home in my flat, nothing to see.

SEA TRIBE

I have seen your yellow butterflies
apparently born of seasky, salt air,
fluttering squadrons
defending doors to other dimensions
between island and island in a sea
northwest of Darwin.
They disappear as they appear: here
among us, then nowhere; an alchemy
of spirit sailed
through sunlight, some enchantment
for a blessed space of sea and time.

Now the bones of those islands erode
beneath transmigrasi, guns, and tourists
like me. The land's heartbeat is fainter
and last time I travelled, begrudged,
squeezed between sacks of cement,
the butterflies did not greet me.

Wrong season, I suppose – and yet –
it seemed as if a veil of magic had been
captured,
cast away, with dying economies and customs
of dismembered islands, where fishermen
caught

in global nets muttered sullenly, and ghosts
of vagrant butterflies sank beneath oily seas

Some grace drops into my dreams
between dreary islands of disbelief.

> I sail at night on sunlit wings
> my compass set by memory's eye
> of Golden Sea Tribe Butterfly.

UNTITLED

On this summer day that is not
one of the brittle blaring days
but a soft and gentle one,
leaves tremble and twinkle
on the crepe myrtle trees
and red brick gleams like jasper.
Magpies patrol the grass, and doves call
from somewhere in the distance, and it seems
as if such lucky days in a country still lucky
for some, will break my heart.

INDEX OF TITLES

A Bird in the Hand	59
An Aspect of Chronic Fatigue Syndrome with Tropical Light	42
Bemos	65
Bilateral Fractures	47
Bushfire Dreaming	15
Chairman, Community Housing	44
Dementia Fears	60
Dementia Games	53
Diurnal	34
Duty One	39
Duty Two	57
Genetic Longevity	52
Gone	31
In The Stocks	63
My Grandfather	17
Never	16
Never Again	29
Neverland	20
Night Lights	35
Ode To My Feet	48
Oh, Ageing!	50
On This Summer Day (untitled)	93
Quiet	32

Reflections	25
Rose Undaughter	22
Sea Tribe	91
Seapath	62
Sky Driving	90
Sorry	28
Suburban Idyll	33
The Child Remembers	18
The News	45
The Walls Around Australia	43
To Peg, 1944-2002	51
Trees	37
Water Sister	69
Waterbed	27

INDEX OF FIRST LINES

Another Anzac Day	29
As a child she followed Cuchulain	20
As the earth turns / I watch the sun	62
Bad girl says / she's a vampire	39
Circling and recircling	34
Early southern winter, morning northern sky	90
Earth is buried	32
I am 10 years old	16
I have seen your yellow butterflies	91
I listen to Judith Wright's poetry about birds	59
I was expecting her husband	51
I was reading a poem	28
I was the last virgin sacrificed to the crocodile god	69
In case there was to be an event	44
In the street today, there's a kind of music	33
In the year 2020 the media ceased reporting wars	45
Indian laburnum/drops petals in Darwin streets	37
Insomniac wired to a Walkman	35
Mirror, stained glass window, curtains	27

My daughter was a rose as rose	22
My grandfather rocked me wrapped securely	17
My hands unhandily wrapped	47
Now I've seen different dementias	60
Oh evolution, why not devise a mechanism	50
On the pyre on the cross on the bonfire, witch	63
On this summer day that is not	93
Once beloved emerald light	42
Once my feet could twinkle in toe-shoes	48
Shadows / in the new house	25
She never raises her voice	53
She was warm in the water / splashing	18
Stuck in mud in fog in anger	57
The bush burns, animals burn, houses burn, sky burns	15
The quietest moment I can remember	31
The walls around Australia / are long grey waves	43
When all the older males of the family are dead	52
When I first went to Kupang	65

AUTHOR BIO Judith Steele is Australian, currently living in South Australia, but still believing that her spiritual home is in the tropics. She has worked as a public servant, English & ESL teacher, & in the hospitality & cleaning industries. She has studied Chinese & Indonesian languages, & travelled in eastern and central Indonesia. She is co-author (with Moira McAuliffe) of *Fighting Monsters* (Vaughan Willoughby, Melbourne, 1998) & was twice winner of the Dymocks Northern Territory Red Earth Poetry Prize (2001, 2002). Her poetry or prose has appeared in Northern Territory & South Australian publications, in *Gobshite Quarterly* (Portland, Oregon), *Tema* (Zagreb); & in webzines including *The Animist, Tinta 3d, & Merida Review*. Her "Testament of harm done to you because of being a woman" appeared in Yoko Ono's project *Arising*, Reykjavik, Iceland, October 2016 to February 2017.

☞ Look for these Reprobate/GobQ titles:

El Gato Eficaz /Deathcats, Luisa Valenzuela (winner 2019 Carlos Fuentes Prize), tr, Jonathan Tittler (en-face bilingual ed.), ISBN: 978-1-93566-234-1 $13

☙

Americá the Beautiful & other indictments (a meaningful life 2.0, txt-only, ed.), Christoph Keller ISBN 978-1-64764-361-4 $10.00

☙

the words I own, michael shay, ISBN 978-1-68454-468-4

☙

The Art of Waking Up; 62 Poems & a Song of Despair (Rev, 2nd ed., incl. recent poems), Brenda Taulbee, ISBN: 978-1-68454-469-1 / / $12

☙

The Jesus He Deserved, & Other Thoughts on War & on Returning, Sean Davis, Matthew Robinson, & Jacob Meeks, ISBN: 978-1-64204-581-9 $14

☙

A White Concrete Day; Poems, 1978 — 2013, Douglas Spangle (2nd ed.), ISBN: ISBN 978-1-62847-660-6 $12

☙

Breakfast; 43 Poems, Coleman Stevenson, ISBN: 978-1-938844-65-4 $12

☙

i'M Afraid of AMericans stories, M F MCAULIFFE, shoegaze books,
ISBN 978-1-944441-5-5 $13.00

☙

SEATTLE; a novella, M. F. MCAULIFFE, shoegaze books, ISBN 978-1-944441-5, $12.00

International trade distrib. through Ingram Spark

☙ ☙ ☙ ☙ ☙ ☙ ☙ ☙

look for special chappy projects & other textual marvels fr. 2020 & beyond.

—◦O◦—

Goshite Quarterly no. 33/36, Winter/Spring 2020, $12

(avail. online & through var. independent bookstores; issues #19/20 & after distrib. internationally through Ingram Spark/Lightning Source POD)

www.ingramcontent.com/pod-product-compliance
Lightning Source LLC
LaVergne TN
LVHW011847060526
838200LV00054B/4213